# MY LISTOGRAPHY

## MY AMAZING LIFE IN LISTS

CREATED BY LISA NOLA
ILLUSTRATED BY NATHANIEL RUSSELL

CHRONICLE BOOKS
SAN FRANCISCO

Text © 2008 Lisa Nola.
Illustrations © 2008 Nathaniel Russell.
www.listography.com

Design by Annie Tsou.
Manufactured in China
ISBN 978-0-8118-6399-5

Chronicle Books endeavors to use environmentally
responsible paper in its gift and stationery products.

10 9

Chronicle Books LLC
680 Second Street
San Francisco, California 94107


www.chroniclebooks.com

# CONTENTS

No ONE ELSE GETS TO BE YOU, AND YOU PROBABLY KNOW THAT YOU ARE TERRIFIC, SO WHY NOT KEEP A BOOK OF LISTS TO CAPTURE WHO YOU ARE? LIST YOUR HOPES, YOUR FAVORITES, AND YOUR GOOD TIMES, BECAUSE YOU MIGHT FORGET WHAT THEY WERE DOWN THE LINE.

I CREATED LISTOGRAPHY SO YOU CAN KEEP A RECORD OF ALL THE LITTLE THINGS THAT ARE IMPORTANT TO YOU; IT'S YOUR AUTOBIOGRAPHY IN LISTS. AND MY FRIEND NAT DID THE ILLUSTRATIONS — WE HOPE YOU LIKE THEM.

SHARE YOUR LISTOGRAPHY WITH YOUR FRIENDS AND FAMILY — OR KEEP IT AS YOUR OWN PRIVATE CREATION. THIS IS YOUR TIME CAPSULE!

AND YOU CAN CONTINUE THE LISTOGRAPHY PROJECT ONLINE : WWW.LISTOGRAPHY.COM.

ENJOY!

LISA NOLA

FRANCINE

# LIST YOUR FAVORITE FRIENDS

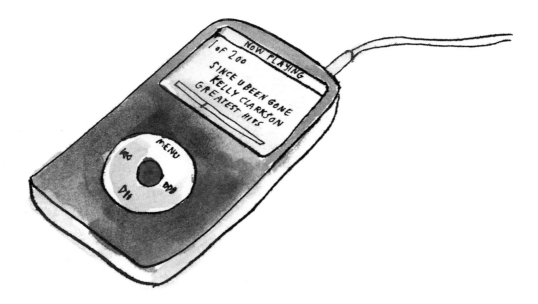

# LIST YOUR FAVORITE SONGS

PRESIDENT

# LIST ALL THE JOBS YOU MIGHT LIKE TO TRY SOMEDAY

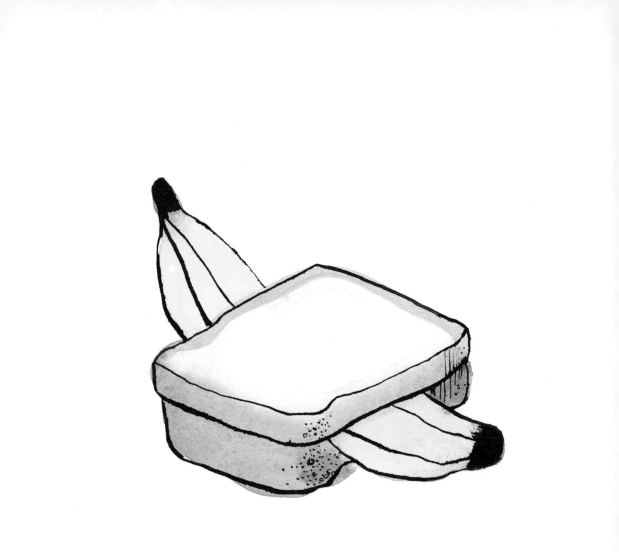

BANANA SANDWICH

# LIST YOUR FAVORITE FOODS

SWIMMING

# LIST YOUR FAVORITE THINGS TO DO IN YOUR FREE TIME

# LIST YOUR FAVORITE MOVIES

# LIST YOUR FAVORITE NAMES FOR GIRLS & BOYS

JOHNNY DEPP

# IF YOU COULD BE FRIENDS WITH ANYONE, LIST WHO

DES MOINES!

# LIST ALL THE CITIES YOU'VE BEEN TO

MR. WHISKERS

# LIST PETS YOU'VE HAD AND THEIR NAMES

# LIST WHAT YOU WOULD DO IF KIDS WERE IN CHARGE

PAUL   RINGO

GEORGE   JOHN

THE BEATLES

# LIST YOUR FAVORITE BANDS OR SINGERS

# LIST YOUR FAVORITE BOOKS

CONFUCIUS

# LIST PEOPLE YOU WOULD LIKE TO MEET

AT MIME CLASS

# LIST THE TIMES YOU'VE HAD AN AUDIENCE

WHEN I BROKE
GRANDMOTHER'S VASE

# LIST THE TIMES YOU GOT IN THE MOST TROUBLE

UNCLE MAX

# LIST THE PEOPLE YOU LOVE MOST
## IN YOUR LIFE

DANIEL RADCLIFFE = HARRY POTTER

# LIST YOUR FAVORITE TV OR MOVIE STARS

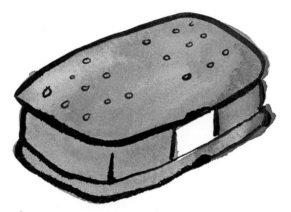

NEOPOLITAN ICE CREAM
SANDWICH

# LIST YOUR FAVORITE SNACKS OR TREATS

MY TOTALLY AWESOME
SKATEBOARD

# LIST YOUR FAVORITE THINGS YOU OWN

BROCCOLI IS GROSS

# LIST THINGS YOU DON'T LIKE

INVISIBILITY

# LIST THE SUPERPOWERS YOU WISH YOU HAD

PARIS, FRANCE

# LIST ALL THE PLACES YOU'D LIKE TO GO SOMEDAY

SOCCER

# LIST YOUR FAVORITE SPORTS

MY FIRST CAMERA

# LIST YOUR FAVORITE GIFTS

EVERYBODY HELPS OUT

# LIST YOUR FAVORITE THINGS ABOUT YOUR FAMILY

OPRAH

# LIST THE PEOPLE YOU ADMIRE

I WISH I COULD FLY

# LIST 10 WISHES YOU WANT TO COME TRUE

PALM BEACH

# LIST PLACES YOU HAVE BEEN ON VACATION

I LOANED STEPHEN MY COAT
WHEN HE FORGOT HIS

# LIST NICE THINGS YOU'VE DONE FOR OTHER PEOPLE

ICE CREAM SUNDAE
FOR BREAKFAST

# LIST WHAT WOULD HAPPEN IF YOUR PARENTS LEFT YOU ALONE FOR A DAY

THE PARK

# LIST YOUR FAVORITE PLACES TO GO IN YOUR HOMETOWN

THERE WOULD BE A PLACE WHERE
ALL THE PETS COULD PLAY TOGETHER

# LIST WHAT YOUR PERFECT WORLD WOULD BE LIKE

I DREAMED I HAD A PET DINOSAUR

# LIST YOUR MOST MEMORABLE DREAMS

GHOST WITH A HAT ON

# LIST WHAT YOU'VE BEEN FOR HALLOWEEN

BUILD A ROLLER COASTER IN THE BACKYARD

# LIST WHAT YOU WOULD DO IF YOU WON A MILLION DOLLARS

# LIST YOUR FAVORITE PLACES TO EAT

# LIST YOUR FAVORITE TV SHOWS

TWISTER

# LIST YOUR FAVORITE GAMES

I WOULD MAKE
MYSELF A LITTLE
TALLER

# LIST THE THINGS YOU WOULD LIKE TO CHANGE IN YOUR LIFE

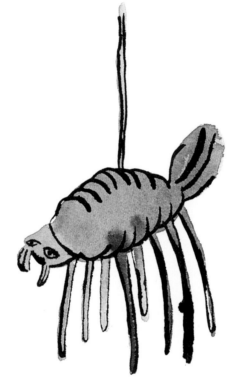

SPIDERS

# LIST SCARY THINGS

P.J.

# LIST YOUR CRUSHES

JUSTIN HELPING ME WITH
MY MATH HOMEWORK

# LIST NICE THINGS PEOPLE HAVE DONE FOR YOU

PETEY

# LIST THE THINGS YOU ARE THANKFUL FOR

BADHAIRCUT.COM

# LIST YOUR FAVORITE WEB SITES

LAST DAY OF 6<u>TH</u> GRADE

# LIST YOUR FAVORITE DAYS SO FAR

WHEN THE DOG ATE MY
HOMEWORK

# LIST YOUR WORST DAYS SO FAR

MORE BIKES

FEWER CARS

# LIST THINGS YOU WOULD CHANGE
## IN THE WORLD

LEARN TO HANG GLIDE

# LIST ALL THE THINGS YOU WANT TO DO
## WHEN YOU GROW UP
### (YOUR LIFE TO DO LIST)

I CAN DO THE SPLITS!

# LIST ALL THE GREAT THINGS
## ABOUT YOU!

MAKE YOUR OWN DRAWING FOR IT

# MAKE YOUR OWN LIST

BEST
&
WORST

BEST SONG SO FAR:

_____

WORST SONG SO FAR:

_____

BEST FRIEND SO FAR:

_____

WORST FRIEND SO FAR:

_____

BEST TRIP SO FAR:

_____

WORST TRIP SO FAR:

_____

BEST GRADE SO FAR:

_____

WORST GRADE SO FAR:

_____

BEST TEACHER SO FAR:

_____

WORST TEACHER SO FAR:

_____

BEST TV SHOW SO FAR:

_____

WORST TV SHOW SO FAR:

_____

BEST DAY SO FAR:

_____

WORST DAY SO FAR:

_____

BEST MEAL SO FAR:

_____

WORST MEAL SO FAR:

_____

BEST GIFT SO FAR:

_____

WORST GIFT SO FAR:

_____

BEST DAY AT SCHOOL SO FAR:

_____

WORST DAY AT SCHOOL SO FAR:

_____

BEST GAME SO FAR:

_____

WORST GAME SO FAR:

_____

BEST MOVIE SO FAR:

_____

WORST MOVIE SO FAR:

_____

BEST _____ SO FAR:

_____

WORST _____ SO FAR:

_____

BEST _____ SO FAR:

_____

WORST _____ SO FAR:

_____

BEST _____ SO FAR:

_____

WORST _____ SO FAR:

_____

BEST _____ SO FAR:

WORST _____ SO FAR:

BEST _____ SO FAR:

WORST _____ SO FAR:

BEST _____ SO FAR:

WORST _____ SO FAR: